POETS WITH MASKS ON

As compiled and edited by

Melanie Simms

Art by

Christine O'Connor

Finishing Line Press
Georgetown, Kentucky

POETS WITH MASKS ON

Copyright © 2022 by Melanie Simms
ISBN 978-1-64662-730-1 First Edition
All rights reserved under International and Pan-American Copyright Conventions. No part of this book may be reproduced in any manner whatsoever without written permission from the publisher, except in the case of brief quotations embodied in critical articles and reviews.

Publisher: Leah Huete de Maines
FLP Editor: Christen Kincaid
Cover Art: Christine O'Connor
Cover Design: Elizabeth Maines McCleavy

Order online: www.finishinglinepress.com
also available on amazon.com

Author inquiries and mail orders:
Finishing Line Press
P. O. Box 1626
Georgetown, Kentucky 40324
U. S. A.

Table of Contents

Preface ix

The Pandemic Poems

"Still Life" *Ellen Bass* 1
"Say this isn't the End" *Richard Blanco* 2
"A Consolation of Chickadees" *Catharine Clark-Sayles* 5
"The Nightly Howl" *Catharine Clark-Sayles* 6
"Forecast for Heat and Riot" *Catharine Clark-Sayles* 7
"The 1918 House" *Gary Fincke* 8
"How to Survive the Pandemic: A Litany" *Gary Fincke* 10
"Los Angeles, February, 2020: The Palm Pruner Explains his Work"
    Gary Fincke 13
"Worship" *Gary Fincke* 14
"Kneading the Bread While Dying" *Christine Gelineau* 15
"A Lamb in May" *Damian Hey* 16
"The Hermit and the Proving Ground" *Damian Hey* 18
"Friends Wear Masks!" *Marilyn Kallet* 19
"Letters from Earth and Sky" *Marilyn Kallet* 21
"After Auden, After Brueghel" *Marjorie Maddox* 23
"False Face Society Masks" *Marjorie Maddox* 24
"Liberty Quarantined" *Marjorie Maddox* 25
"Pronouns" *Marjorie Maddox* 26
"Take Me OUT to the Ball Game..." *Marjorie Maddox* 27
"During Stay-at-Home Orders, Our Son Cuts My Husband's Hair"
    Marjorie Maddox 28
"Inside" *Marjorie Maddox* 29
"Where We Can't Walk" *Gary Margolis* 30
"Turning On Your Screen" *Gary Margolis* 32
"Beer Pong with Masks" *Gary Margolis* 34
"In the Virtual Waiting Room after Elizabeth Bishop" *Gary Margolis* 38
"Fake Crowded Noise" *Gary Margolis* 41

"Trace the Curve *for Lori Lightfoot*" Ariana Moulton 43
"Lean In" *Ariana Moulton* 44
"Below the Peak" *Ariana Moulton* 45
"Papilio Glaucus" *Jason O'Toole* 46
"Last Nights" *Jason O'Toole* 47
"Hello Lovebirds" *Molly Peacock* 51
"Like a Panther: Covid 19 Isolation Exercise" *Molly Peacock* 53
"Food shopping on the Eve of Self-Isolation, a Love Poem"
    Molly Peacock 54
"Disinfection Dance" *Molly Peacock* 55
"Today my Mask is the Codicil" *Molly Peacock* 56
"Proceed with Caution" *Connie Post* 57
"Living the Days of Corona" *Connie Post* 60
"Covid-19 Shelter in Place" *Connie Post* 62
"Guidelines in a Pandemic" *Connie Post* 63
"Not Yet" *Monica Prince* 64
"The First Day" *Monica Prince* 65
"Things I Wish I Had but Don't *after Alejandra de la Cruz*"
    Monica Prince 66
"In Our Time of Plague" *Bertha Rogers* 67
"Mother's Ashes" *Melanie Simms* 68
"Owl" *David Swanger* 69
"Debate Cut Up" *Robert Sward* 70
"Hide and Seek" *Jesse Waters* 71
"Ash" *Jesse Waters* 72

Acknowledgements 73

The Poets 75

Preface

I could never have imagined sitting at a library in Northumberland, PA (current county Covid-19 case count, 1,893 as of today), compiling a book about a world-wide pandemic. And yet, it occurs to me that there is no compilation more effective to do so than that of a collection of poetry written by some of America's finest poets today.

Poets, throughout time have been our witnesses through mankind's greatest trials and achievements because of their ability to provide emotional connectivity and healing through unified reflection; during our current Covid-19 crisis, we need that connectivity even more so.

Before this book began, it was a germ of an idea that was planted by a question posed to me by a well-known local radio host in Sunbury, PA Mark Lawrence of WKOK. During an interview in March of 2020. One of his questions on that show set a fire within; "so how do you think this pandemic will change your writing? Do you think the pandemic might also change the landscape of the poetic field in some way?"

I realized then and there that I had yet to significantly contribute anything about the pandemic, though some of my colleagues had already begun posting poems about it on Facebook, or had already realized their own publications of pandemic poems in the usual run of well-known literary journals.

I decided that my response and personal contribution was to create a pandemic anthology. I knew that to do so I would certainly need enough poets to drive the book forward, and so I began asking poets from all walks of my life if they would contribute. I reached out to old mentors from my younger years in Santa Cruz, California (David Swanger, Ellen Bass, Robert Sward) and to those I had met along my journey as an undergraduate at Bloomsburg University and in Wilkes-Barre, Pa. including Marjorie Maddox, Christine Gelineau and Molly Peacock. I was truly blessed to have gathered such a wealth of friends in the poetry field.

Fortunately, most of those I asked poems of agreed (including many talented poets I had connected with on Facebook). I am equally honored and grateful to include in *Poets with Masks On*, many of America's finest poets both from not only my home state of Pennsylvania ,but nationally as well. This book grew to include, also, the pandemic poems of Richard Blanco, Connie Post and Marilyn Kallet, as well as more well-known Pennsylvania poets Gary Fincke, and the ever-talented Marjorie Maddox. There are many any other fine names you will no doubt recognize if you are familiar with our field.

Some of these poets contributed one poem, others had multiple poems to share so you will notice this derivation. This is not a judgement on who this author deems more worthy to express the pandemic through their eyes. It is simply a matter of availability.

During the process I found myself depressed at times. Having to slow the project down to catch my own breath, though fortunately not from the experience of acquiring Covid, writing during a pandemic can stifle one's creativity and increase a level of anxiety that makes it hard to flourish as an artist.

This book is more to me than just a pandemic collection. This book is a loving creation put together by friends and colleagues who saw the need for this project and championed me to create this so that we might have a document of these times, expressed through the competent lens of the American poet.

I wish us all a safe and healthy passage as we navigate Covid-19 in our darkest times here in the United States and abroad. May this book serve as a testament to those times. May we never forget.

Melanie Simms
(Snyder County, current Covid-19 case count 651)

Christine O'Connor

Still Life
(by Ellen Bass)

It won't last,
of course. The sun

at just this angle
on the coral tulips. Even now
they're spinning away, but oh,

these open mouths reach out
on their supple stems,
revealing yellow throats, golden
pistil and black anthers wheeling.

They ride the air, louche cups of emptiness,
satin feathers, parrot-colored curtains, they billow,
they plume, dreamy sails, slack bells, they lift
and tremble at the slightest shift, even my breath
sets them nodding. For a minute,

maybe two, they
dwell and crest,
then the planet's stream
takes them with it
and the shallow pond of light is gone—

except the tip of one petal
still catching the sun

Say This Isn't the End
(by Richard Blanco)

… say we live on, say we'll forget the masks
that kept us from dying from the invisible,
but say we won't ever forget the invisible
masks we realized we had been wearing
most our lives, disguising ourselves from
each other. Say we won't veil ourselves again,
that our souls will keep breathing timelessly,
that we won't return to clocking our lives
with lists and appointments. Say we'll keep
our days errant as sun showers, impulsive
as a star's falling. Say this isn't our end …

… say I'll get to be as thrilled as a boy spinning
again in my barber's chair, tell him how
I'd missed his winged scissors chirping
away my shaggy hair eclipsing my eyes,
his warm clouds of foam, the sharp love
of his razor's tender strokes on my beard.
Say I'll get more chances to say more than
thanks, Shirley at the checkout line, praise
her turquoise jewelry, her son in photos
taped to her register, dare to ask about
her throat cancer. Say this isn't her end …

… say my mother's cloudy eyes won't die
from the goodbye kiss I last gave her, say
that wasn't our final goodbye, nor will we
be stranded behind a quarantine window
trying to see our refracted faces beyond
the glare, read our lips, press the warmth
of our palms to the cold glass. Say I won't
be kept from her bedside to listen to her
last words, that we'll have years to speak
of the decades of our unspoken love that
separated us. Say this isn't how we'll end …

… say all the restaurant chairs will get back
on their feet, that we'll all sit for another
lifetime of savoring all we had never fully
savored: the server as poet reciting flavors
not on the menu, the candlelight flicker
as appetizer, friends' spicy gossip and rich,
saucy laughter, sharing entrées of memories
no longer six feet apart, our beloved's lips
as velvety as the wine, the dessert served
sweet in their eyes. Say this is no one's end …

… say my husband and I will keep on honing
our home cooking together, find new recipes
for love in the kitchen: our kisses and tears
while dicing onions, eggs cracking in tune
to Aretha's croon, dancing as we heat up
the oven. Say we'll never stop feasting on
the taste of our stories, sweet or sour, but
say our table will never be set for just one,
say neither of us dies, many more Cheers!
to our good health. Say we will never end …

… say we'll all still take the time we once
needed to walk alone and gently through
our neighborhoods, keep noticing the Zen
of anthills and sidewalk cracks blossoming
weeds, of yappy dogs and silent swing sets
rusting in backyards, of neat hedges hiding
mansions and scruffy lawns of boarded-up
homes. Say we won't forget our seeing
that every kind of life is a life worth living,
worth saving. Say this is nobody's end …

… or say this will be my end, say the loving
hands of gloved, gowned angels risking
their lives to save mine won't be able to
keep me here. Say this is the last breath
of my last poem, will of my last thoughts:
I've witnessed massive swarms of fireflies

grace my garden like never before, drawn
to the air cleansed of our arrogant greed,
their glow a flashback to the time before
us, omen of Earth without us, a reminder
we're never immune to nature. I say this
might be the end we've always needed
to begin again. I say this may be the end
to let us hope to heal, to evolve, reach
the stars. Again I'll say: heal, evolve, reach
and become the stars that became us—
whether or not this is or is not our end

A Consolation of Chickadees
(by Catharine Clark-Sayles)

"Rats" my neighbor says. She found a nest
beneath the old doghouse but blames spilled seed
from my bird feeder across the fence.
Because she writes a note and seals it in an envelope
I take the feeder down and feel a little guilt
at chickadees in cold rain at my windowsill.
Through the winter frosts I spread a morning cup
along the rail and it is gone before rat hour.
Today roses and honeysuckle seduce the bees,
I pour in seed and hang the feeder back,
the neighbor won't be pleased but—quarantine—
Third month of viral fear, I need my birds.

The Nightly Howl
(by Catharine Clark-Sayles)

at 3 AM the world goes quiet, no trains to doppler by.
The 8 PM howl every evening since March sparse to night—
most howls I give three barks and feel one small light
sparked against a blackness part despair, part rage—
the social righteousness of three months ago, a stage
moved through like Londoners in the early blitz
determined not to yield, but how long—when hits
keep coming: deaths from virus and injustice rise,
cities burn, histories and statues topple, politicians' lies
wind into sticky webs with truth a shriveled carcass
pushed into the corner of the news. The harvest?
None can say, but sleep becomes the price tonight.
Pen, paper, scribbled words—I tell myself I will be all right.

Forecast for Heat and Riot
(by Catharine Clark-Sayles)

Ninety-one today, basil droops
revives with sprinkles from the hose—
pizza and pesto essence floats
with bees, following the promise
of mock orange, lavender and Jeanne
LaVoie to their blossomed reward.
Yellow-dusted they bumble back
visit tomato blossoms on the way;
somehow it all gets sorted and green
marbles grow on apple trees
cluster tangles of tomato vines
bursting from their cage,
this small square of world
pulls bare toes to dig fragrant soil.
I imagine roots, turn my face to sun
breathe out the burden
of a country caught in flames.

The 1918 House
(by Gary Fincke)

My father, whose limp is a stutter,
Says he was born in the epidemic,
The early days, when people survived
Like expected because it was just flu.

In May, he tells me, the cases were
Three day fevers. By June, he says, the flu
Had moved to where it always summers,
Far from the warm weather of families.

My father, who shuffles like those who
Are stared at by children, accepts my hand
For surfaces other than sidewalks
To examine every place where he's lived.

In September, he tells me, symptoms
Meant death—the coughing of blood, the blue face,
The darkening of feet that said "soon"
In the common language for conclusion.

The lungs, he says, went soggy with blood,
The people drowned for days. The newly born,
He murmurs, were passed over like sons
Of Jews, God's mercy on our infant breath.

My father, who refuses a cane,
Touches a wall he built in a yard owned
By strangers, pausing on his way to
The beginning, the house where, in the year

Of the Spanish flu, he was first-born
And no one died, where his parents survived
To see themselves chosen, praising God
And good fortune and their lifetimes of work.

On both sides, he says, are the houses
Of victims, sons who enlisted for war,
And he pauses, the porch so different
I have to read the number to prove it.

How winter blessed us, he says, ending
That horror, driving us inside to love.
He asks me to knock on the white door;
He says these people will invite us in

How to Survive the Pandemic: A Litany
(by Gary Fincke)

Practice cough etiquette—
a tissue or your inner elbow,
never your palm.

This is the other side of stone

Avoid touching
your eyes, your mouth, your nose.

This is the other side of water

Begin social distancing,
closing schools and day cares.

This is the other side of walls

Elsewhere, avoid crowds.

This is the other side of screens

If that is impossible,
maintain distance from others.

This is the other side of names

Beware rumors and fake news.

This is the other side of eyes

When things worsen, isolate yourself
and your family inside your home,
practicing "shelter in place."

This is the other side of doors

Be sure to have cached
at least two weeks
of water, food, and medicine.

This is the other side of future

To minimize contact
with the sick in your home,
designate a room for quarantine.
This is the other side of comfort

Wear a filter mask if you need to.

This is the other side of flesh

Buy the masks ahead of time
because there will be a shortage.

This is the other side of story

A new vaccine will take months.

This is the other side of fear

Remember that those
at greatest risk will receive it first.

This is the other side of jealousy

Get to know your neighbors
because you will need their help.

This is the other side of intimacy

Don't let fear erode empathy.

This is the other side of prayer

In the last great pandemic,
the sick often starved to death
because those still healthy
were terrified to go near them.

This is the other side of beginning

Los Angeles, February, 2020: The Palm Pruner Explains his Work
(by Gary Fincke)

First, sterilize every tool. Soak them in bleach mixed one to three with water.

"Soak" means five minutes minimum. To sterilize the chain saw, remove the chain and bar and immerse both pieces. The same goes for the hand saw and knife. Rinse them with water. Air dry.

Climbing the tallest palms means learning to use a harness and cables. Spiked shoes should never be used. They will permanently damage the trunk.

Use the chainsaw for the large fronds, but care needs to be taken. Saw them close to the trunk, but do not cut the trunk. Cuts never heal. They will leave the tree defenseless.

Pull the boots by hand. Never attempt to saw them off. If they do not pull easily, leave them.

Do not use the tools on another palm tree without disinfecting. Never forget that diseases are easily spread by dirty cleaning tools. Where we are, fusarium wilt is the most likely. The lower fronds turn yellow, wilt and die. The upper leaves rapidly follow. At last, a few surviving fronds will form a spike at the top of the tree, but by now the entire plant is dying.

Once a tree is infected, there is no cure.

Worship
(by Gary Fincke)

As everyone at your zoom meeting begins the odd goodbyes of isolation, Denise says, "Would you like to see our butterfly collection?" None of the eight face-filled panels blacks out. Denise tilts her laptop so the camera shows the dining room wall behind her is nearly covered with hung boxes of butterflies. You count twelve, nine in each box. 108 butterflies that look identical to you.

"It's our best wall," Denise says. "They come dry in the mail, then Harry moistens them and fixes them in place. He builds all the boxes himself." She has never mentioned the butterflies at the meetings before the lockdown. You search the faces in the panels, looking for a match to your wonder. Two panels go dark.

"We're just getting started," Denise says. She stands, the room swaying through her camera. She carries the laptop closer to the wall. All of the butterflies seem to have the same deep blue with golden specks in a simple, consistent pattern. "They have names," Denise says, beginning a slow pan across the boxes. "If I turned these frames over, you'd see them on the back. They're all the same species, but more like cousins than brothers and sisters."

Four panels are dark. "Harry is in self-quarantine," Denise says, but so far, he's fine. He has a new set to keep him occupied. He is so incredible with the tweezers and pins and the syringe." She moves her laptop closer to the wall, holds it steady. You think of an atlas you once owned, how the biggest cities were enlarged in panels. "We have so many walls," Denise says. "The butterflies are raised on farms. They are plentiful. Eventually, we'll be surrounded. Don't these look well-cared for? Don't they look as if they could fly?"

You are alone with Denise. This virus will bring you back to her dining room for months, or longer, another wall sprouting something like an ivy of boxes. What she will show, and you will call beauty's still life while those others who meet with you go quickly dark into their ordinary, private lives.

You vow to look up the species. To ask her now seems taboo, an interruption of worship. You imagine Harry busy with a new specimen, carefully restoring something dry and fragile under a brilliant light. While you stare and stare, all that is left of Denise is breathing.

Kneading Bread While Dying
(by Christine Gelineau)

Not a loaf from antiquity forward
has ever been formed by hands
that were not dying—it's not
that I've forgotten that, but here
I refer to the special quality imbued
to the feel of the yeast springing alive
under your palms when the breadmaking
is an attempt to distract yourself
from the Covid symptoms that
that have flared, and receded, flared
and receded within you now for weeks.
At 3 a.m., pacing, jittery, bellowing
your lungs in deep five-second breaths,
you find yourself pondering what
a life means, living, what is
the import of new mornings
when the darkness surrounds you
elementally as oxygen?
Remember that time on the plane,
the pilot preparing you for
emergency landing, twenty
minutes until we are "on the ground,"
see you on the ground
the pilot said and you curled into
yourself, folded into stasis, unable
to imagine what could one ever do
equal to the last twenty minutes of your life,
a question you knew even then had no answer.
And now, the window of time left
less definite, you fill the hours:
walk out into the cold spring
to breathe the chill air and visit
the nodding daffodils, or you FaceTime
the grandchildren, or you knead
the living dough, hands pressed deep
into the rising warmth of our daily bread

A Lamb in May
(by Damian Hey)

Roberta was a rhapsode and a blasphemer.
A lamb for weeks, she wouldn't talk to anyone
then one day, in the recreation area,
she'd rise from bingo, arms outstretched, proclaiming

I,
who am beloved,
strike the stars
to smash the chains of heaven
at the cuffs

And I,
who am incarnate,
blast the bones
to purge the marrow
of the hallowed dead.

You shut your stupid mouth, Roberta, someone'd shout,
and Benjamin or Anthony—or both—would come
to gather her and calm her down and give her meds.
And off she'd go, a silent little lamb, again.

And I,
who am forsaken,
played a prank,
and sent a godless
man to lead the world,
and scores of righteous fools
to deem him holy.

And then I,
who am anointed,
sent a scourge—
two hundred thousand dead,
and still evangelists
would deem him holy,
offering their praise
and gratitude

This outburst came not long into election year,
and we'd lost fifteen residents in just one month.
Henrietta Bishop, Christian to the core,
had told her rosary, "He's such a saintly man!"

Now I,
who am empowered,
raise the roof
and tell my people:
I am not your friend.
My father's business
is no longer mine,
and he has gone away
I don't know where—
In any case, it's none
of my concern,
nor none of yours.

Roberta never had another word to say.
It came in March.
Roberta died, a lamb, in May.

The Hermit and the Proving Ground
(by Damian Hey)

I lived apart through early Spring—
a brutal calculus in the air,
my world was close,
and dead,
and full of dying.

I went inside to try my faith—
a darkened rosary in my hand,
my prayer was sharp
and keen,
and long of keening.

I cloistered through the Summer's months—
an unsure oracle in my brain
its vision short
of time
and off in timing.

I weather this pandemic Fall
a single sacrament at a time—
a tedium
of ends
and never ending.

I haven't born the Winter, yet—
a doubtful terminus to an age—
a proving ground
of hope
and yet of hoping.

And should the ague have no end,
I'll make mete offerings day to day—
for all who have
endured,
and are enduring.

Friends Wear Masks!
(by Marilyn Kallet)

"Excuse me," the moose tapped the goose,
"Why aren't you wearing a mask?"

"Why do you ask?" replied the goose.
"Because these are scary times, bad germs

on the loose. So we protect each other
by covering our noses and mouths."

"But I'll look ugly," said the goose.
"No, you'll look like you're ready

for a costume party," said the moose.
"Your eyes are your best feature,

my friend!" But the goose was
clueless. "Real men don't wear masks,"

he said. "They should," said the moose.
"Germs don't know who's ripped, who's

Dem or GOP. Real men protect their
fams, and we are one people, we are kin.

"Do it for me!" begged the moose,
"Or you will be a silly, sickly goose."

"Okay, okay," said the goose, "for you,
I'll cover my nose and mouth.

Because we're pals. And though
we're different, we both

love Knoxville, that's the truth!"
"Thank you," said the moose, to his

healthy, wise friend. They stayed pals to the long-lived end!

Letters from Earth & Sky
(by Marilyn Kallet)

The petals
on the earth
and William Stafford
say it best:
You are not alone.
The dogwoods
stand, jays screech
improv
with the hawks.
Yesterday,
the neighbors'
black Lab
came racing by
for a caress,
and you could hear
your own
shameless
heart.

So wrap yourself in
hope & a mask
and walk—greet
that family at
the end
of the block.

Silky
petals
drop
like divine notes,
& no one
gets
hurt—be
like that,
soft,
kind.

Read that tiny
ant-memo, crawling
on your glasses
while you write:
You are not alone.

Rimbaud
was wrong: I
is not "someone else."
I is all of us,
on a stroll to meet
the new, the guileless,
and the oldest
blossoming trees—

long-flowering ones
we yearn to sing
& become.

After Auden, After Brueghel
(by Marjorie Maddox)

> "About suffering they were never wrong,
> The Old Masters…" W. H. Auden, *Musée des Beaux Arts*

There is no turning away from this,
or there is, the sandy-toed raising a glass
to the Atlantic's deep blue forever
just as Icarus plunges (or Brueghel's Icarus,
or Auden's memory of Brueghel's Icarus),
a memory of a memory of someone else's suffering:
just incidental peripheral on a bright day of hangovers
until the undertow tugs down the neighbor
they may know slightly from,
in some other season,
skating at the edge of the wood,
or petting their doggy dog,
or even lining up beside them
for the miraculous birth,
which, too, may be cancelled
along with any resurrections
if the day is predictably sunny,
the landscape ready to plow or paint,
and the stubborn wind,
just in from a tsunami,
distracted enough for a sail.

False Face Society Masks
(by Marjorie Maddox)

—*Joy of Museums Virtual Tours, May 2020*

For this mask: not hallowed horsetail but
my own hair—now coronavirus style—
auburn and gray, frizzed, flopped over
the elongated features of fear—
ancient eyes, deep-set; nose bent
by the diseased scent of death—
dark-grained face chiseled and cut
from the living trees in the woods
where we've wandered
too long.   Too long we've wandered
in these woods, invoking the disfigured
and hunchbacked, our fractured pleas
crying out for that healing Iroquois spirit,
"Old Broken Nose," who once tried
to move mountains, but, distracted,
looked back and, slapped on the cheek by stone,
ran off to hide his shattered countenance
in a cave. "Come out," we pray,
"and save us!"   But the woods,
are just a screen we're scrolling
on this virtual journey to nowhere,
the familiar cautionary tale interrupted
by the latest digital specter—
ironic black-and-white advertisement
for colorful masks: soft cotton, machine-washable,
available—today only—in a wide variety
of "reasonably priced" and "highly authentic"
new-age Native-American designs.

Liberty Quarantined
(by Marjorie Maddox)

—virtual tour, May 2020

Outside,
at last, here,
I want to be inside,
at last, there, and I am,
not across the choppy bay or
too tired at the base with a stroller
and two toddlers, but clicking and turning,
high-stepping up all those 154 steps, then scaling,
even in my too obedient past prime imagination, all
305 feet, then—touting ultimate freedom—up and into
the off-limits since 1918 thinly coated 24K gold flame *O say can you see*
me here at home—stretched out in the fenced-in backyard,
cyber-traveling—but also there *by the dawn's early light*
way before official operating hours *once upon a time*
when the world still operated *we hold these truths*
O *give me your tired* say can you *your poor,* see
Your tired masses yearning at the tiptop
of the world on fire *to breathe free*
even here at the bottom, *wretched*
refuse even here, *homeless,*
homebound, even
here.

Pronouns
(by Marjorie Maddox)

—*May 2020*

"Time out!"
says the young mother to the toddler
        too loudly,
pretending a scream is not a scream.

The small girl stands in a corner
crowded with fear. She flails her arms,
then settles her tear-streaked face
into a pout.
        Outside, the sun dazzles
without her.
                It is her mother she hates,
the one digging now through the kitchen trash,
what's left of the mask soiled with coffee grounds,
Elmo safety scissors hidden deeper yet
beneath the last egg shells, the empty carton of milk.
        Outside, the sun dazzles
without them.
                The mother cuts her finger
on a discarded can. The daughter wails.
Someone is screeching, "Out! Out! Out!"
She is/is not the child. *She* is/is not the mom.
        Outside the sun.
                Without them.

Take Me OUT to the Ball Game...
(by Marjorie Maddox)

    –Summer 2020

The stands now emptied of *them*,
there's nothing really here:

no bellows, no pantomimed blows,
even jeers and middle fingers a missed memory.

But worse: only the weight of breath
rounding the bases, dust not thick enough

to hide absence. Only exaggerated taunts
of uniformed rivals, half-hearted, really,

fizzling into sighs. Spitting, high-fives,
celebratory tackles—all foul

of what's acceptable, the dugout
a den of masks and dread.

Each hot, dry night, the heave
of the team pushes through innings

where hip-hips once slipped into
overwhelming hoorahs, Sweet Carolines

no longer curling lips into *bah-bah-bah!*
To be tagged Out would be better than this

erasure of Safe, would be touch, would be
before, would be being again outside

the single silent gaze of the camera.

During Stay-at-Home Orders, Our Son Cuts My Husband's Hair
(by Marjorie Maddox)

The division of before/after
begins again: indoor/outdoor,

the backyard wild with weeds,
the hum of clippers angling along

the overgrown lawn of my husband's scalp.
Our child/adult, too young to remember 9/11,

refuses fear, keeps his eye and hand steady.
Gray locks float happily down,

settle on a patio that has no memory
of before and why. Now, the student/

turned barber adjusts the razor, circles an ear,
without hesitation, steers confidently

to mitigate the proliferation of beard.
Under the sharp blade of the vibrator,

my husband relaxes,
calmly exposes his neck.

Inside
(by Marjorie Maddox)

One house and this rhythm of ritual:
6:00 a.m., 8:00 a.m., 4:00 p.m.—our laptops open
in the kitchen, the living room, a bedroom,
Hellos at the refrigerator, while ascending/
descending the stairs, the constant tap of keys
the background of faraway horses we're all riding—
professor/parents, one-day professor/son—
across this long expanse of knowledge where we're
kicking up dust *someone goes out for a walk;
someone returns* on our way to a strange horizon
we hope is sunrise. *Good morning.
Good afternoon. Good night.* And we gather
for whatever's unfrozen or freshly baked,
and we watch what makes us laugh or tear up
or say *Proud of you. Love you. Thank you.*
And one stays up all night writing essays.
And two wake up early grading essays.
And everywhere there is typing and Zoom.
And on the morning and the evening
of the forty-second day, there is much darkness,
but also light. And it was good.
It was still good.

Where We Can't Walk
(by Gary Margolis)

Thoreau didn't have to cross
places off his list.
Like us.

The trail around the pond.
The long road back to Boston.
Nor did Dickenson, who loved

her room more than a path
in the woods.
Who walked in circles
around her desk.
Stevens took the same sidewalk
to work.
Thinking
of blackbirds and jars,
the bars in Key West.
Cummings never thought

to stay inside.
And strolled with his spaces
and commas around

Harvard Yard.
Kumin and Sexton worked
on revisions together.

Pushing strollers around
Newton.
Never bringing up Plath

in front of their children.
Whom they wished had taken
a walk instead.

Often a good medicine.
When desire is the desire
not to go anywhere.

No one's saying with any
confidence
how long this will last

in New England.
The staying inside.
The masks.

Reading our poets.
Say Wheatley.
Who walked away

from her chains.
Say Phyllis Wheatley,
her married name.

Say her name
for as long as you can.
Circling a pond

with your neighbors.
That pole walker,
across the way.

Who's hard to recognize.
Even with the mist
burning off.

Turning On Your Screen
(by Gary Margolis)

Granddaughter, I know it isn't good
for you and all the country's children
to watch so much television.

To pretend walking to school
by turning on your screen.
To wave at your teacher,

your friends at this distance.
Some mornings, to mute yourself,
so no one can hear

what you're feeling. Such sadness
you don't know how to say it,
to keep it in its pencil box.

September's meant for other things.
Tracing leaves. Standing with your
friends, at recess, at the far end

of a paved yard, under the shedding
maple tree. It's okay
if you want to shout

at the brick building,
I can't stand this. I hate my t.v.
If you're sick of all of it.

The promises of what's to come.
How things are sure to get better.
Which is what I'm telling you too

granddaughter. Raking my leaves
from here, deeper in the country.
A pile, you can see, as tall

as a building, for you and your sister
to jump into and disappear.
To rise from, when all is said

and done. With all of that glitter
in your hair. Fall's confetti.
It might take you all night

to brush out. So you can be
ready for tomorrow's school day.
Pretending to stand on the sidewalk,

waiting for the school bus.
Looking back, up at your bedroom
window. Your mother's waving from.

Beer Pong With Masks
(by Gary Margolis)

You're not sure it's up to you
to deputize yourself, walk over
to that old fraternity house.

To engage those boys, those men,
to raise their masks. Like flags.
To not drink so much beer,

they have to lower their scarfs
more often than what's good
for you and your neighbors.

The neighborhood their house
resides in. What would you be
doing, fifty years ago,

on a fall Saturday afternoon?
Studying? Going over your class
notes? Sitting in the library?

More likely watching a game
from the stands of a stadium.
Or, if you were lucky, walking

with another freshman, a girl,
through a local orchard. Stepping
over the drops, beginning

to get to know each other.
Drinking a glass of sparkling,
spiked cider. From a flask?

A go-cup? Not paying much
attention to the yellow jackets.
Not worrying about kissing,

in those days. And the dreaded
mononucleosis. A virus
that could keep you in bed

or too many days of your first
semester. I know isn't the same
as what you're facing now

in the throes of the pandemic.
Even here at your small college
in autumn's country.

Of leaves. Of apples. Of students.
Trying to have their full
experience. Living away from

home. From worrying parents.
All the decisions there are
to make. Like yours.

Whether to stay inside your car
and not say anything
at what you're seeing.

Now that they're more
than four beer-pong,
drinking players.

Word must have gotten out.
There's a party going on.
And no football game to go to.

No orchard they know of yet.
Just new friends living on the edge
of a town's neighborhood.

Call it an assembly.
What else would you expect,
remembering your own memories.

Expect of yourself now.
To call campus security?
To step out of your car,

with your mask up?
To walk across their lawn
with a bushel of apples?

Christine O'Connor

In the Virtual Waiting Room after Elizabeth Bishop
(by Gary Margolis)

No National Geographics.
Pamphlets, soft toys
or toy boxes.

No receptionist or nurses.
No other patients,
save me, alone,

in my own room.
Waiting for the doctor.
Calling, it might seem,

from some room
in his house.
Perhaps, some place,

he, too, is alone.
To ask how are you?
How have you been?

Has anything changed
since the last time
we talked, we met,

in person, at the end
of an afternoon?
With time to exchange

a few uninsured words.
That day before
everything changed.

And we were asked,
were told to stay in.
When in-was-home.

An alley. A park bench.
A house on a quarantined
street. When a city

of offices closed.
And you—I mean you
and me—doctor and patient—

had to find
a new way to say
what it is hurting.

To sort through symptoms
and mystery.
How it is to see

each other
on a screen.
No matter how long

we've known
each other.
Whether this is an emergency

or, more likely, a routine
appointment.
Without a magazine

to pass the time,
to calm the anxiety.
Of the war down the street.

The virus there's no shot for.
What Elizabeth, the girl,
the woman might have written.

Her ghost. Her lines we can
read in our mind's eye,
our body's anthology.

And not on our time's
diagnosed screen.
You and I waiting,

let's presume,
to check-in.
To still know

who we are—
Is it you? Is it me?—
As we appear.

Fake Crowd Noise
(by Gary Margolis)

Piped-in call of the beer
vendors.
Leather-on-wood
crack of a ball

on its bat.
The flag clanking
the center field pole.
Even the batter

cursing under his breath.
Swell of a cheer
cresting like a wave
circling the park,

a stadium, a field.
Neil Diamond's
Sweet Caroline
swaying the seventh

inning's stretch.
By any stretch
of the imagination
Any recorded sound

to fill the emptiness.
To make it seem
as if we are here.
Listening. Unaware

of what's lost.
What's surrounding us
is gone.
Call it ambient noise.

A crowd's voice.
What's hard to live,
to play without.
Never wanting

to think of a game,
a national pastime,
playing inside
an echo, an echo

chamber
of peanuts and beer
and souvenirs
here. My friends,

the real sound
of masked
police cracking heads
beyond the wall.

Trace the Curve *for Lori Lightfoot*
(by Ariana Moulton)

What if someone told you
you couldn't go where you normally go?
Would the *you* in you come undone?

Not seeing what you expect to see.
You're not alone in your quarantine,
except you are, globally masked, tightly tonight.

Would you even know if someone rearranged your desk at work,
moved your ruler aside, borrowed your protractor
and traced the curve we aim to flatten?

It's these flat lands where the wind sweeps for miles,
I see in my sleep, particles like dust.
Keeping us awake, watchmen of an invisible enemy.

If you've never been told no then how would you know
you wouldn't go back there, to that place you're supposed to be?
You would have grabbed more of your things, that ruler.

How could you measure freedoms of the past you've never lost?
Until this moment, when Madam Mayor quotes a poet,
Ms. Brooks herself, calling upon us to cultivate *'dreams in the dark'*.

It's bigger than us, microscopically and
'it wants to crumble you down, to sicken you'.
Your words bring us all, to a place where gold will attach itself

as we breathe freely tonight.

Lean In
(by Ariana Moulton)

Drinking coffee black as iron,
the expectant teacher, still quarantined today.
My class dings digital doorbells,
this checkered screen,
ancillary attendance.

Ariel's corner square holds two.
A smirk, a smile, a younger face so dear.
Come near, who are you?
Your cousin leans into you,

to hear our daily schedule,
to see us sign the Pledge of Allegiance.
Her allegiance shown in her snuggle,
her need to connect, you protect.

I only hope I'm opaque enough in this moment
to block news feeds, fed with anger,
while Minneapolis screams for Floyd,
for innocent iron souls,
my role, to welcome, to protect our visitor.

A six-year-old whose Wi-Fi must have been down,
whose mother's essentially working.
Come in, I'll read to you of an imaginary
mouse who's searching for his lost love.

It's only love that can save us all
from concrete fractures,
a century of flames that have licked liberally
against you.

Below the Peak
(by Ariana Moulton)

In New Hampshire,
the seniors rode up a ski lift to graduate,
no skis or heavy boots to swing.

Each chair hung safely distanced,
far enough for gowns to dance above
naked trails.

I imagine a crackled Pomp and Circumstance
called from the lodge,
moving them to set victory.

To wait their turn,
extend an eager hand,
disinfected diplomas.

I've never walked off
a chairlift so lifted with
accomplished breeze.

Did they throw their hats
into a flock of ravens that day,
a furried flutter?

Time must have come for them to descend,
to choose a trail, black diamond,
blue circle.

It's not easy to remember one
ride up the mountain
when your eyes are flooded with change

and tassels tell the story,
unwritten, your future
below the peak.

Papilio Glaucus
(by Jason O'Toole)

Sparrow's beak tore free
band of blue spots,
ripped slit
through yellow wings,

framing pine needles
on verdant branch,
she swoons.

She doesn't die here
& was last seen
flying above the canopy
against a summer sky.

Last Nights
(by Jason O'Toole)

Passing in the stairwell,
no eye contact
nor situational awareness.
Am I not a potential threat;
so evidently housebroken
& tame?

In her billowy wake:
aroma of air freshener,
dryer sheets, fresh kitty
litter
& abstinence.

Run home little miss,
to sugar-free evenings
of screen time & clean sheets.

Spate of ill fortune!
we'd all retreat inside
ourselves.

Casting protective circles
Twelve feet in diameter
with Lysol & panic attacks.
Swearing, we had not,
ourselves
summoned the invisible principality
nibbling at our mortality.

Into individual serving caves,
watching shadows
flicker on our Samsungs,
uncertain if we'll ever emerge.
Fearful of what expects us
in the broken future.

Enter into a futile passion,
hiding our faces from humiliation
& spitting,
veiling our images:
tattooed skin, boot chipped teeth,
smoker's cough & fatty liver.
Brittle matter
of which we are formed.
Mere shadow of our true spirit.
One hopes.

In ethanol we trust.
Lemony fresh disinfectant wipes
& germy squirt.
Slay the unseen adversary
lurking on every surface
& even
on final notices
slipped under our door.

How unlike the acrid smells
we loved so well,
of blithe nights
long past.

Stink of hot knives
in Tompkins Square.
Shoplifted French perfume
haunting art school corridors
lined with bad student drawings.

Clove cigarette smoke permeates
each indelicate memory.
Mouthfeel of too many
espressos
& puffs
from hastily rolled joints.
Joints rolled
on subway seats.

Ladies in peril
of their own design.
Cut their own bangs,
& messed it up
every time.

First dates in graveyards
& last dates ending
in fistfights
with her old boyfriend.
Purine beer from cloudy taps
in bars not carding girls
who can't be fifteen,
bouncing in laps of skinheads
with raw knuckles
& angel dust stares.

Rent party, nobody knows
who lives in this loft.
Sweating under painted leather.
Dancing in her bra
stuffed with street money.
Unwashed hands dip cups into
punch spiked with Absolut & ecstasy.

Tiny kitchen, failed attempt
at Vietnamese cooking,
her fish sauce breath upon you.
Split lips kissing
after vomiting vodka drinks.
Nobody held her hair
in the vandalized bathroom.

Manic Panic head
stains pillowcase blue.
Using your toothbrush
spitting out hippy toothpaste
not approved
by the American Dental Association.

Nights sullied, magnificent
dying with you & me
limping into the awful
eternity of tomorrow.

HELLO, LOVEBIRDS
(by Molly Peacock)

"Hello lovebirds!" The newbie nurse
says to us, entwined in a hospital bed,
(our island rectangle on a gray floor sea)
in this Covid Era in the cancer center,
on a limited four-hour visit that still
is boring (because there's nothing extra,
not even a plant in the room),
so, we're streaming an Irish love story.
On the island of the screen, the soft-faced
actors-in-love talk at agonizingly
cross purposes—oh we know how that felt.
We broke up at that age, too.

"I'm going to interfere with your manliness,"
the nurse says, raising a navy-blue
plastic razor, like a miniature oar.
She needs to shave a patch of chest hair,
thick and curly as seaweed,
so the heart monitor pads will stick.
Stymied, she leaves to get scissors
as scenes of Trinity College Dublin fly by.
We recognize it from all our visits
after we collided again as grownups.

"I haven't done this before," our nurse returns,
clips the seaweed patch on the beach of chest,
and dips the blue-oar razor in a paper cup of water.
We are fine today, by the way—he's not in pain.
Decades unroll behind us like seafoam—
what happened to Anxiety and Fear?
(Evaporated into the atmosphere…)
Using a tiny navy-blue oar to lift seaweed hair?
Pitifully ineffective. "We've got some shaving cream,"

HELLO, LOVEBIRDS!,
I say. (We travel equipped.) Of course!
The green-blue gel foams up, the hair parts,
the sticky heart patch attaches to his skin,
and we all congratulate ourselves as she wafts out.
Each actor lies in a narrow bed at night alone
with a tiny bright rectangle of a cell phone.
We broke up from our dorm rooms holding
heavy, short-corded turtle-shaped phones
with rotary dials like tillers, twelve recurrences ago.
On the screen, from his bed raft, he picks up a lit cell.
She has texted him.

LIKE A PANTHER: COVID 19 ISOLATION EXERCISE
(by Molly Peacock)

> *... paces in cramped circles, over and over*
> Rainer Maria Rilke, *The Panther*
> Translated by Stephen Mitchell

Marching ten steps across the balcony,
times one hundred…Beyond, occasional traffic blurs
the railings, so now they're cage bars, skinny
iron stripes that deaden the eye the way
Rilke's panther lost its soul—wasn't it just
a cat, standing in for a poet, a way
to talk about being trapped? The zoo bars' rust
and the twists of the panther-taunters' faces…
the inhumane reigned… All this laces my self-talk
a thousand paces toward the panther,
as walking in isolation pitches me back,
the present collapsing to the past
where now, a child, I live inside a Great Cat.
It's not just something standing in
for something else looming.
A panther is blooming.

FOOD SHOPPING ON THE EVE OF SELF-ISOLATION, A LOVE POEM
(by Molly Peacock)

Broccoli, apples, pears, potatoes,
sturdy survivors. Ignore those tomatoes
(they'll never last the indefinite time
we'll have to self-isolate). Grabbing lime,
lemons to zest and preserve, like friendship.
We customers move without speaking and slip,
no bumping, tight-aisled automatons on our
vegetable track, before the market hour
is done, and we lumber home to cook…
all our speed behind us, careers forsook
all getting ahead ridiculously dead—
what were we thinking, rushing and linking,
when home is the only safety and tea
(glad it's obtainable!) and water (yes, still potable)
makes us sit down (after we wash our hands).

You and me on the couch holding hands.

DISINFECTION DANCE
(by Molly Peacock)

Think of it as glitter,
sick-sparkles to expunge,
invisible countertop litter
erased in jittery swipes.
Think of it as glitter,
our lives saved by a sponge.

TODAY MY TASK IS THE CODICIL
(by Molly Peacock)

Contemplating life being over
in the panic weeks as the triage of the ill
sorts the ones like me to die… I must accept
being passed by: I've had my pomegranate life.
Seeds sluicing red…. Rose affection.
Vermilion dread. The juice: friends of fifty years,
you in your sweat-pants and virus mask.
Crisp gold type on a black, matte folder.
Like 81% of those over
the age of 72, I have one:
Will. Just one vowel away from being well,
as we are now. But today my task is the codicil
that designates the little stuff: a paperweight, a watercolor,
six leather volumes of Mrs. Delany's letters,
typed in a Docx. to send to Wills and Trusts,
so a healthy stranger, young and un-
known to me now, will see to what she must.

Proceed with Caution
(by Connie Post)

Assume
everything is contaminated

assume every surface
you touch
holds an invisible illness

you can spread it
without knowing

you are asymptomatic
but everyone
turns away

they can tell
that fear mutates
as quickly as a virus

the earth
whispered in your ear
long ago
"I will find you
I will find a way
to tell you when I've had
too much"

so you spend your days
looking for your own
antibodies
you search for them
in the soil
where you know
you will someday return

you sanitize your thoughts

you don't say anything to anyone
but you've had a sore throat
for fourteen days

the earth is having trouble breathing

there are no more ventilators

Christine O'Connor

Living the days of Corona
(by Connie Post)

The numbers change
by the hour
I check the web site
too often

I tell myself not to
watch the news
all the time

I wipe down my counter
instead

after dinner
I find a new graph
on the trajectory of deaths
in my region

I watch the curve spike
and see small images of people
falling off the back

like that scene in
Titanic
when everyone
fell off the ship

some to the ocean
some to the decks below

some plummeting
some holding on
some lonely
when the water
froze their stories in time

I try to sleep
all my meditation songs
fall below my bed

someone is being infected
someone is short of breath
someone remembers a prayer
they said when they were young

COVID 19 Shelter in Place
(by Connie Post)

Don't get me wrong
The corona virus is
making its way through the world
with its own fury

at night I lay awake
and shudder about
all the suffering
my daughter keeps coughing
and I don't settle into sleep until dawn

but there is something else happening
behind the scenes
a friend you haven't heard from in a while
reaches out and asks if you are okay

people smile at the grocery store
while not touching
Baseball games and concerts are cancelled
but the poets still write

I watch the same movie four times
with my grandson

we stay in more
remember a long-ago vacation
and make popcorn with real butter

we enjoy every morsel of pancakes
and a sandwich with the crust cut off

The virus
how long will it stay with us
how long will we remain
both distant
and isolated
while the earth
shows us the way

Guidelines in a Pandemic
(by Connie Post)

Don't touch anything
not the doorknob
nor elevator button
or the jagged space
between
your cleaved lungs

wear a mask
to protect others
wear a mask
to hide your cyanotic self
the blue of your lips
the exact hue
of the ocean
we've smothered

don't let the
dead whale's carcass
float too close
to your bed

the small bits of plastic
inside the remains
will remind you
of dying
with plastic in your body

as if they
were trying to tell
their own story

and the body bags
washing up to shore
were not our own

Not Yet
(by Monica Prince)

If this is the end, let there be unbroken sunlight
so everyone experiences the tunnel the same way.

If this is the end, let every avocado be ripe enough
for toast, guacamole, smoothies, and rice bowls.

If this is the end, may my beloved's lips trail philosophy
of magnetism against my skin, conjuring theories of what
our lives could have been had we loved each other a little harder.

I will not ask for more time, not even mercy.

If this is the end, I want to dance naked in the street,
yes, barefoot with blue nail polish on, even if it's raining,
especially so, my hair be damned, because I always held such
resentment for precipitation like water ever wanted
to drown her own baby.

If this is the end, paint me extravagant against my house,
making love where everyone can see us while they are too busy
smuggling pleasure for themselves to care.

I want to scream, rip pages out of books,
scatter them like blessings on the wind.

Let the fires come, let the mountains collapse,
let the waves run into our arms at full speed.

If this is the end, remember there was suffering,
and pain, and deep injustice—but there was also
so much light, a song written in our bone marrow,
love I never got to understand but vibrated in fiercely.

When it all grinds to a halt with a whisper on the tongue,
know that I made what space I could beautiful, deliciously mine.

The First Day
   (by Monica Prince)

On the first day I can do the splits
in all three directions, I will wear
a dress with pockets and do the splits
on every lawn between here and my lover's house.

On the first day I can run
three miles without stopping or walking,
I will run on the track at the university
wearing a tank top and booty shorts
that say *POETRY* on the butt because that day
I'll be poetry in motion.

On the first day I no longer have to lesson plan
for a semester that feels oh so weary,
I will buy outdoor furniture and sip mojitos
while reading a book I don't plan to teach.

On the first day I wake up without a nightmare
chasing my consciousness, I will throw
a massive block party and use my savings
to rent a bouncy castle so we can all witness
freedom inside our own chests—buoyant, up, up, up.

On the first day pandemic is over,
I will get my vaccine, wash my hands,
pet a stranger's dog, wash my hands again,
and drive nonstop to Colorado to hug my mother.

On the first day this body elicits unedited joy
in the mirror, I will kiss her in every place my lips can reach,
whisper, *I love you, I love you, I love you.*

Things I Wish I Had But Don't
after Alejandra de la Cruz
 (by Monica Prince)

Nail polish that never chips.
A live-in housekeeper. Speakers in every room.
My office on campus. A working microphone
on my personal laptop. More flexibility—
in my hips, thighs, back, heart.
A tubal ligation. Monday night wings
with a rotating group of my favorite people.
Soundproof walls. The ability to watch
Game of Thrones without yelling about racism,
sexism, or the British. To never Zoom again.
Time to write—really write, spend six hours
huddled in a comfy chair while my partner
brings me tea and occasionally eats me out.
Better oral sex skills. A bigger bed.
Three partners I could actually see, hold,
kiss. A proper pedicure. Unlimited gin.
New sex toys. Sunshine with no clouds.
A Susquehanna River clean enough
to drink from, fish in, float away on.
More gratitude, less despair,
the end of pandemic, lockdown, and unfair.

In the Time of Plague
(by Bertha Rogers)

Masked, we know
only
each other's eyes;
the words we think
lost to mumblings.

We are disguised.
We are what we see—
hair, shoulders, coated arms,.
the criminals
we used to catch.

Shielded from each
other's truth,
what we perceive
as smiled greeting
is hate, layered—
our dearest enemy.

One day, the shrouds
will untie
themselves,
leave
our battered skulls.

We will die into
crowded backgrounds—
trees at last,
happily robbed of leaves.

MOTHER'S ASHES
(By Melanie Simms)

Emilio takes me down Interstate 40
From Albuquerque to the Painted Desert
To spread my mother's ashes.
I hold them in my lap, sealed
In a red Scottish whiskey tin.

She made me promise
To spread them into the sky
Of the Painted Desert
So she could be free,
Floating over the Arizona Mesas
Of the desert sand.
I love Emilio
For driving the long way
He doesn't have to do this.
"She's your mother," he says.
"We have to honor her spirit."
(I'd kept her ashes for years in the cupboard
In the kitchen).
I don't want to let go. I wanted to
Wake up each morning knowing
Some part of her remained.

We reach the desert, park his truck and make the hike to spread her ashes,
Walking towards the white vermillion cliffs;
Crossing petrified rock and dinosaur tracks;
(The remnants of an ancient world that still calls out from the past).

In the Mesa, we see the petroglyphs
Carved in stone. I can see
Why mom asked to be freed here.
Everything here is sacred.
Emilio helps me open the tin
And the wind carries my mother across the desert.

Owl
(by David Swanger)

The owl, the most silent flier,
who flies on the softest feathers,
sees by the smallest moonlight
the vole, the mice among grasses,
and the rabbit. In the owl quiet,
in the owl shadow, those who are
left await their turn. The owl is
someone in a white coat in a room.

Debate Cut-Up
(by Robert Sward)

Operation warp speed. The production and delivery of 300 million doses of a safe and effective vaccine to control the Corona virus-19 by January 2021
warp 9 corresponds to 900 billion kilometers an hour,
830 times the speed of light.... travel restrictions apply, safe and effective vaccines,
"we were able to..." who aggressive, Plexiglas, 21,000 dead bodies a day,
2500 Dr. Fauci, safeguards, we were able to, super spreader events,
we were able to produce and deliver, operation warp speed, we did everything, safe and effective vaccines, confidence, hard work and prayers and concerns, right to know the reality, blue collar workers, Biden will not... climate change is an existential threat, 100,000 jobs, two trillion dollar tax bill, Biden will not ... 200,000 Pew Poll... the reality is... 1.8 billion dollars, which I'm trying to do... the Supreme Court, the reality is 8 minutes and 40 seconds, equal Justice, which I'm trying to do, George Floyd America is basically racist, Breonna Taylor, Because it's vibrating, seems. Solid, because it's vibrating, Look we always see 21,000 dead bodies, Dr. Fauci, Breona Taylor

Hide and Seek
(by Jesse Waters)

On her 57th birthday
from her bed
in the living room
my mother teaches
an imaginary kindergarten class.

They sit in their chairs
sing back a happy song and snack
on chocolate wafers. At recess
they cover their eyes
count to 100...
their hands tap each
other on the shoulder.

And run around in circles!

Afternoon comes. Everyone
lies down for naps.
I touch my mother's blouse, and close
her attendance book. Outside,
the air brakes
on a small, yellow
bus shriek.

Ash

(by Jesse Waters)

I barricade myself with smoke
and in one lung a simple thing

turns black. The word 'silhouette'. What
does the body make of its need

to know where being finally goes?
When we're done it's said we're off to

something more. But what if here, day
and night is really back from where

we were, and now, finished, where we
so want to go. It's hard to live

one year. It's hard to live a long,
long life no matter where your roots

when all we need is something less
of light. Just a bit of less when we're through

with what was us. Now, even in shade, my shadow
still stands though I can't see it. I follow myself in

and out of light, longer as I reach
a place I'd always meant to be.

Acknowledgments

I wish to thank the following individuals for their contributions towards the creation of *Poets with Masks On*; artist Chris O'Connor, ever-inspirational radio host Mark Lawrence, two of my favorite libraries The Rudy Gelnett Library in Selinsgrove, PA and the Priestly-Forsyth Library in Northumberland, Pa. Christine Gelineau for encouraging me to pursue this collection when I wasn't sure it would be the right project for me or that it would excel. I also wish to thank my many friends, mentors and colleagues for rushing to my aid and submitting their gifted contributions of poetry; to *all of you*, thank you so much.

Please note that some of the poems included in *Poets with Masks On* have been previously published. Below are their publication credits:

Ellen Bass's "Still Life," was previously published in *Together in a Sudden Strangeness,* edited by Alice Quinn.

Richard Blanco's "Say this isn't the End" was previously published in *The Atlantic.*

Gary Fincke's "The 1918 House," was previously published in *The Gettysburg Review* and Gary's own collection, *The Fire Landscape.* His poem, "How to Survive a Pandemic: A Litany" was previously published in his new collection, T*he Mussolini Diaries.* Prose poem, "Los Angeles, February 2020: The Palm Pruner Explains his Work," was also included in *The Mussolini Diaries* by Gary Fincke. "Worship" was previously published in *Atticus Review.*

Christine Gelineau's "Kneading the Bread While Dying," first appeared in *Rattle.*

Marilyn Kallet's "Friends Wear Masks," first appeared in the City of Knoxville's webpage. It was composed for Mayor Indya Kincannon at her request.

Marjorie Maddox's poems "After Auden, After Brueghel," "During Stay-at-Home Orders, Our Son Cuts My Husband's Hair," "Inside," "Liberty Quarantined," and "Pronouns" appear in her book *Begin with a Question* (Paraclete Press 2022), as well as elsewhere listed below. "Pronouns" also appeared in *2020 An Anthology of Poetry with Drawings by Bill Liebeskind,* ed. Judith S. Bauer, Black Dog & One-Eyed Press and in *San Diego Reader.* "After Auden, After Brueghel" appeared in *Artists and Poets Respond to the Pandemic: An On-line Exhibition,*

San Diego Review, and *Pandemic Poetry,* Headline Poetry and Press. "During Stay-at-Home Orders, Our Son Cuts My Husband's Hair" and "Inside" were published by *MER VOX*, whereas "Liberty Quarantined" was published in *The Plague Papers* at *Poemeleon: A Journal of Poetry*, as well as by Silver Birch Press' Landmark Series. Her poem "False Face Security Masks" appeared in Silver Birch Press' Wearing a Mask Series and *The Ekphrastic Review*. Finally, "Take Me OUT to the Ballgame..." was previously published in *Aethlon: The Journal of Sport Literature.*

Connie Post's poems were all published previously in *CaliFragile.*

Melanie Simm's poem, "Mother's Ashes," was previously published in her book collection *Remember the Sun,* by Sunbury Press.

David Swanger's poem, "Owl," was previously published in *5_Trope.*

The Poets

Ellen Bass's newest book, *Indigo*, was published by Copper Canyon Press in April 2020. Among her previous books are *Like a Beggar* (2014), *The Human Line* (2007), and *Mules of Love* (2002). With Florence Howe, she co-edited the first major anthology of women's poetry, *No More Masks!* (1973). Among her honors are three Pushcart Prizes, The Lambda Literary Award, The Pablo Neruda Prize, Larry Levis Prize, *New Letters* Prize, and Fellowships from the NEA and the California Arts Council. Her poetry appears frequently in *The New Yorker, The American Poetry Review,* and many other journals. Bass is also coauthor of the groundbreaking *The Courage to Heal: A Guide for Women Survivors of Child Sexual Abuse* (1988, 2008) and *Free Your Mind: The Book for Gay, Lesbian and Bisexual Youth and Their Allies* (1996). A Chancellor of the Academy of American Poets, Bass founded poetry workshops at Salinas Valley State Prison and at the Santa Cruz County jails, and she teaches in the low-residency MFA program in writing at Pacific University. www.ellenbass.com

***

Selected by President Obama as the fifth Presidential Inaugural Poet in U.S. history, **Richard Blanco** is the youngest and the first Latino, immigrant, and gay person to serve in such a role. Born in Madrid to Cuban exile parents and raised in Miami, cultural identity characterizes his many collections of award-winning poetry, including his most recent, HOW TO LOVE A COUNTRY, and his memoir THE PRINCE OF LOS COCUYOS: A MIAMI CHILDHOOD. Blanco is a Woodrow Wilson Fellow, has received numerous honorary doctorates, serves as Education Ambassador for The Academy of American Poets, and is an Associate Professor at FIU.

***

Catharine Clark-Sayles is a geriatrician practicing north of San Francisco. She travelled across the United States extensively with a military family while she was young, then became an Army doctor. When she turned forty she discovered that she had missed her twenties the first time around and reconnected with poetry to find them. She has published two books of poetry with Tebot Bach Press: *One Breath* in 2008 is poetry drawn from medical training and practice. *Lifeboat* was published in 2012. Recent work has appeared in *Spillway, Locuspoint.org, The Squaw Valley Review, Persimmon Tree, The Healing Art of Writing*, vols.1 and 2.*Neat, The Healing Muse*, many of annual *The Marin Poetry Center Anthology* and *The Poetry Farmer's Almanacs*. After a military-brat childhood of frequent moves across the United States, she attended college and medical school in Colorado then moved to Northern California in 1979 for medical training as an Army physician. Better as a doctor than as a soldier she chose civilian life and a private practice specializing in older adults. Dr. Clark-Sayles has learned poetry by reading and working with mentor poets Margaret Kaufman, Robert Sward and David St. John.

***

Gary Fincke is a poet and author of short fiction and nonfiction. Born and raised in Pittsburgh, Pennsylvania, Fincke earned his BA from Thiel College, his MA from Miami University, and his PhD from Kent State University in 1974. He began his literary career that same year and has published over 20 works. He is the recipient of multiple awards for his poetry, including the Bess Hokin Prize from *Poetry* magazine and the Rose Lefcowitz Prize from *Poet Lore*. His collection *Writing Letters for the Blind* (2003) won the 2003 Ohio State University Press/*The Journal* poetry prize. His prose work has also earned him various honors, including the Flannery O'Connor Award for Short Fiction in 2003, a PEN Syndicated Fiction Prize, a George Garrett Fiction Prize, a Lewis Prize for Nonfiction, and two Pushcart Prizes, among others. In a review of Fincke's memoir, *The Canals of Mars*, for *Pank* magazine, Salvatore Pane noted Fincke's "laser-accurate observations" and "keen sense of rhythm and metaphor." Fincke is a professor Emeritus of Susquehanna University in Selinsgrove, Pennsylvania, where he also served as the director of the Writers Institute. He lives with his wife in Selinsgrove.

***

Christine Gelineau is a poet and essayist and the author of three full-length collections of poetry: *Crave* (NYQ Books, 2016), *Appetite for the Divine* (Editor's Choice for the McGovern Publication Prize, Ashland Poetry Press, 2010) and *Remorseless Loyalty* (Ashland Poetry Press, 2006), which was awarded the Richard Snyder Memorial Prize, and which was subsequently nominated for the *Los Angeles Times Book Award*. Gelineau's other books include two chapbooks of poetry, as well as the anthology *French Connections: A Gathering of Franco-American Poets* (Louisiana Literature Press, 2007).

Gelineau's poetry, essays and reviews have appeared in or been accepted to numerous journals and anthologies, including: *Prairie Schooner, The New York Times Opinionator, New York Quarterly, Connecticut Review, New Letters, The Iron Horse Review, Green Mountains Review, Georgia Review, Paterson Literary Review* and others, and have appeared on Verse Daily and Poetry Sunday (Women's Voices for Change). Her poem "Sockanosett" won a Pushcart Prize in 2013. Three of her essays have been cited as "Notable Essays" in *Best American Essays* ("Foal Watch" in 2004, "The Gift That Cannot Be Refused" in 2007, "Courtesy of the Gravedigger" in 2015), while her essay "Cops" was the runner-up in the 2009 *Florida Review* Editors Award in Creative Nonfiction. Gelineau lives on a farm in upstate New York. She holds a Ph.D. in literature with a creative dissertation in poetry and essays from Binghamton University.

***

Damian Ward Hey has had poetry published in several places, including Poetry Pacific, Truck, and Cricket Online Review. More recently, his work has appeared in Madness Muse Press and will appear also in an upcoming issue of Cajun Mutt Press. He lives on Long Island and is a professor of literature and theory at Molloy College.

***

Marilyn Kallet recently served two terms as Knoxville Poet Laureate. She has published 18 books, including *How Our Bodies Learned, The Love That Moves Me,* and *Packing Light: New and Selected Poems,* Black Widow Press. She translated Paul Eluard's *Last Love Poems* and Benjamin Péret's *The Big Game.* Dr. Kallet is Professor Emerita at the University of Tennessee. She mentors poetry groups for the Virginia Center for the Creative Arts, in Auvillar, France. Her poetry has appeared recently in *New Letters, One, Thrush* and *North American Review.* Poetry is forthcoming in *Cutthroat, 101 Jewish Poems for the New Millennium,* and *New Voices,* an anthology confronting antisemitism.

***

Winner of *America Magazine*'s 2019 Foley Poetry Prize and Professor of English and Creative Writing at Lock Haven University, **Marjorie Maddox** has published 13 collections of poetry—including *Transplant, Transport, Transubstantiation* (Yellowglen Prize); *True, False, None of the Above*

(Illumination Book Award Medalist); *Local News from Someplace Else; Perpendicular As I* (Sandstone Book Award)—the story collection *What She Was Saying* (Fomite Press); four children's and YA books—including *Inside Out: Poems on Writing and Reading Poems with Insider Exercises* (Finalist Children's Educational Category 2020 International Book Awards), *A Crossing of Zebras: Animal Packs in Poetry; Rules of the Game: Baseball Poems*; and *I'm Feeling Blue, Too!—Common Wealth: Contemporary Poets on Pennsylvania* (co-editor); *Presence* (assistant editor); and 600+ stories, essays, and poems in journals and anthologies. Her books *Begin with a Question* (Paraclete) and *Heart Speaks, Is Spoken For* (Shanti Arts) are forthcoming in 2022. Please see www.marjoriemaddox.com

***

Gary Margolis is the author of three books of poems, *Fire in the Orchard, Falling Awake* and *The Day We Still Stand Here*. He is director of counseling at Middlebury College where he is also a part time Associate Professor of English. A recipient of Vermont Arts Council and Millay Colony Awards, and a former Robert Frost Fellow at the Bread Loaf Writers' Conference, his poems and essays have appeared in *Poetry, American Scholar, Poetry Northwest,* and other journals. He lives in Cornwall, Vermont, where he is a volunteer firefighter.

***

Ariana Moulton is a 3rd grade teacher and poet living in Chicago with her two daughters, husband and puppy. She grew up in Cornwall, Vermont. She attended Bates College and has her master's from Columbia College Chicago. She is inspired by nature, politics, Chicago, Vermont, and has been mentored by her father, poet Gary Margolis. Her writing has been seen in *Verity LA, Poet's Choice, Lucky Jefferson, Poem Village, What Rough Beast Covid 19 Edition* and her first manuscript "Trace the Curve" will be published with Atmosphere Press. Ariana has found the pandemic to be a source of will and creativity.

***

Christine O'Connor is an artist from Schenectady, New York. She enjoys working in paint, collage, metal, glass, fiber, and pastels to create wall art, jewelry, and sculpture. She is known for her surprising color combinations and whimsical creations. Christine has shared her love of making art by teaching classes in beading, book making and felting at several venues including the

Arts Center of the Capital District, Boston Chapter of Glass Beadmakers Bead Retreat at Snow Farm, Sunnyview Hospital Recreation Therapy Studio Arts program, Double H Ranch, and her home studio. Her work has been shown at The Sprinkler Factory, The Veiwpoint Gallery, Saratoga Arts Center, and Zion Lutheran Church. It is also inthe private collections of many artists and on permanent display in the Viewpoint Gallery, Schenectady, New York.

***

Jason O'Toole is the author of two poetry collections, Soulless Heavens and Spear of Stars and has been featured in over a hundred anthologies, journals and newspapers. His poem "Samsara" which debuted in The Scrib Arts Journal, was nominated for the Science Fiction & Fantasy Poetry Association's Rhysling Award. He is a member of the North Andover Poet Laurette Committee.

***

Molly Peacock (born Buffalo, New York 1947) is an American-Canadian poet, essayist, biographer and speaker, whose multi-genre literary life also includes memoir, short fiction, and a one-woman show. Peacock's works include *The Paper Garden*, a biography of Mary Delany, an 18th-century gentlewoman and a meditation on late-life creativity. *The Paper Garden* was selected as a book of the year by *The Economist*, which said of the work, "Like flowers built of a millefeuille of paper, Ms Peacock builds a life out of layers of metaphor."[1] Her latest book of poems is *The Analyst*, a collection exploring her evolving relationship with her psychoanalyst who, after a stroke, reclaimed her life through painting. She was a Faculty Mentor at the Spalding University Brief Residency MFA Program, 2001-13. Molly Peacock is also the author/performer of a one-woman show in poems, "The Shimmering Verge" produced by Louise Fagan Productions, reviewed by Laura Weinert in the New York Times. "She can inhabit a moment with quiet intensity: in a haunting poem about an alcoholic father hovering over her, she fully enters her scene, gripping the folds of fabric around her as if they might swallow her alive."She has published seven collections of poetry, including *The Second Blush,* love poems from a midlife marriage and *Cornucopia: New & Selected Poems*. Widely anthologized, her work is included in *The Best of the Best American Poetry 1988–1997* and *The Oxford Book of American Poetry*, as well as in leading literary journals such as the *Times Literary Supplement, The New Yorker,* and *The Paris Review*. Peacock is the author of a memoir, *Paradise, Piece By Piece*. Her essay on Mrs.

Delany, "Passion Flowers in Winter", appeared in *The Best American Essays*. Other pieces appear in *O: The Oprah Magazine, Elle, House & Garden*, and *New York Magazine*. She is also the editor of a collection of creative nonfiction, *Private I: Privacy in a Public World*. As the former President of the Poetry Society of America, Molly Peacock was one of the creators of the *Poetry in Motion* program; coediting *Poetry In Motion: One Hundred Poems From the Subways and Buses*. She was also the Series Editor of *The Best Canadian Poetry in English* (Tightrope Books) from 2008–2017, as well as a Contributing Editor of the *Literary Review of Canada*.

***

Connie Post is a San Francisco Bay Area Poet who has been writing and publishing for over twenty five years. Her work has received praise from Al Young, Ursula LeGuin, Ellen Bass, Maxine Chernoff and former US Poet Laureate Juan Herrera. Her first full length collection *Floodwater* was the winner of the 2014 Lyrebird Award from Glass Lyre Press. Her second full length collection *Prime Meridian* was just released in January of 2020. (Glass Lyre Press). She has two chapbooks from Finishing Line Press *And When The Sun Drops* and *Trip Wires*. Her other books include *Waking State* (Small Poetry Press) and 2 other self-published books about parenting a son with autism Connie Post's poetry has been published widely, including the following publications: *Apparatus Magazine, Adanna, The Aurorean, Arsenic Lobster, Blood Root Literary Magazine, Blue Fifth Review, Barnwood International, Big Muddy, Calyx, Comstock Review, Cold Mountain Review, Chiron Review, Chabot Literary Review, Crab Creek Review, Copperfield Review, Caesura, Clackamas Literary Review Carquinez Poetry Review, California Quarterly, Convergence, DMQ Review, Dogwood, Glint, Iodine Poetry Journal, I 70 Review, Italian Americana, Karamu, Kalliope, Kentucky Review, Lindenwood Review, Main Street Rag, Monterey Poetry Review, Mid West Poetry Review, Mobius, Oberon, Palooka, Pirene's Fountain, Psychic Meatloaf, One* (Jacar Press) *Prick of the Spindle, Porter Gulch Review, Poemeleon, RiverSedge, Rise up Review, Slipstream, Song of the San Joaquin, Snail Mail Review, Spillway, Spoon River Poetry Review, Tipton Poetry Journal, The Toronto Quarterly, The Dirty Napkin, Timber Creek Review The Tule Review, The Pedestal Magazine, The Great American Poetry Show, Wild Goose Poetry Review, Up the Stair Case Literary Review, West Trestle Review, Untitled Country Review, White Pelican Review, Third Wednesday Two Bridges Review, Valparaiso Poetry Review,* and *Verse Daily.*

***

Monica Prince is an assistant professor of activist and performance writing at Susquehanna University, the current managing editor for the Santa Fe Writers Project online journal, *Quarterly*, and a co-owner of the leadership company Your Leadership Recipe in France. Her debut poetry collection, *Instructions for Temporary Survival*, published by Red Mountain Press this June, won the Discovery Award through the publisher for an exceptional first collection. Her choreopoem, *How to Exterminate the Black Woman*, which premiered at Susquehanna University in spring 2018 to sold-out audiences, will be published by the publishing arm of *[PANK]* in spring 2020. She recently completed the 5th Woman Fellowship in Knoxville, Tennessee, where she performed a co-written choreopoem with four other women from the east coast. Monica writes, performs, and works in Selinsgrove, PA.

***

Bertha Rogers has published her poetry in literary journals, anthologies, and her collections, including *Wild, Again* (Salmon Poetry, 2019); *Heart Turned Back* (Salmon Poetry, 2011); and *Sleeper, You Wake* (Mellen), as well as several chapbooks (*The Reason of Trees, A House of Corners, The Fourth Beast,* and For the *Girl Buried in the Peat Bog*). Her translation of Beowulf was published in 2000, and her translation of the Anglo-Saxon Riddle-Poems from the Exeter Book, *Uncommon Creatures*, was published in 2019. In 1992, with her late husband, Ernest M. Fishman, she founded Bright Hill Press & Literary Center of the Catskills; she retired as executive director in 2017 and now serves as Editor in Chief. She serves as Poet Laureate of Delaware County and reads her poetry to audiences throughout the Northeast and abroad.

***

Melanie Simms is a widely published award-winning author. She is a former county poet laureate for Perry County, PA and the author of four books, *Life Signs and Fortune Cookies, Remember the Sun, Waking the Muse* and *Poets with Masks On.* She is the recipient of several awards in poetry including a Richard Savage Award (second place) winner of the Poetry in Transit Award (King's College) and a Vermont Writer's Studio Scholarship. She had appeared on numerous radio and television shows both statewide and internationally including multiple NPR affiliates, PCNTV, a frequent guest on the Mark

Lawrence Morning Show (WVIA) among many others. Her second love is science fiction and she is currently working on her latest novel *Alien Prophecy* and is an avid supporter of NASA and MUFON.

***

David Swanger has published four books of poetry, two chapbooks, and poems in various anthologies and journals. Awards include fellowships from the N. E. A. and the California Arts Council. His most recent book, *Wayne's College of Beauty*, won the John Ciardi Poetry Prize. Currently, he serves as Poet Laureate of Santa Cruz County.

***

Robert Sward has taught at Cornell University, Iowa Writers' Workshop, and UC Santa Cruz. Born & raised in Chicago, Sward served in the U.S. Navy in the combat zone Korean War Era. Produced features for CBC Radio. 1980s, book reviewer & feature writer also for *Globe & Mail* and *Toronto Star* while living on Toronto Islands. He is a Guggenheim and PEN OAKLAND 2020 Lifetime Achievement Award Winner and served as Poet Laureate of Santa Cruz County, 2016-2018.

***

Jesse Waters is currently Director of The Bowers Writers House at Elizabethtown College. His fiction, poetry and non-fiction work has been nominated for multiple Pushcart Prizes, and has appeared nationally and internationally in such journals as *The Adirondack Review, Coal Hill Review, The Cortland Review, Cimarron Review, Iowa Review, Magma, River Styx, Slide, Story Quarterly, Southeast Review, Sycamore Review* and others.

www.ingramcontent.com/pod-product-compliance
Lightning Source LLC
Chambersburg PA
CBHW042145160426
43201CB00022B/2410